Defendant Stephan
Cowans sat in a
Boston courtroom.
He was accused of
shooting a police
officer.

The Evidence

Witness after witness testified against Cowans. Experts claimed that fingerprints found at the crime scene matched Cowans's. An eyewitness had picked Cowans out of a police lineup.

If the jury believed the witnesses, Cowans could go to jail for a long time.

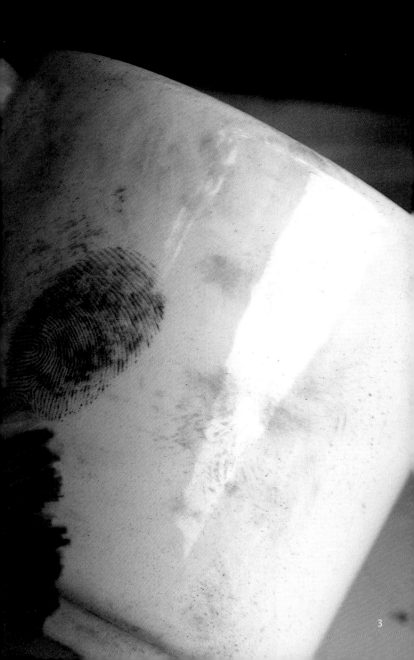

The Verdict

A few days later, the jury returned its verdict. Guilty! Cowans was sentenced to 30 to 45 years in jail.

Still, Cowans insisted he was innocent.

The Question

How would Stephan Cowans ever be able
to make a case for his innocence? When—
if ever—should convicted criminals get a
chance for a new trial?

PREVIEW PHOTOS

PAGE 1: Stephan Cowans, sentenced to prison for shooting a police officer, insisted that he was innocent.

Book Design: Red Herring Design/NYC **Photo Credits:** Photographs © 2012: Alamy Images: 16 (Deco Images II), 37 (ICP), 41 top right (Stockfolio), 2, 3 (vario images GmbH & Co.KG); AP Images: 8 (Mary Altaffer), 27 center right (Bob Child), 27 right (Tom Gannam), 1 (Mark Garfinkel), 34, 35 (Angela Rowlings), 36 (Toby Talbot); Corbis Images: 40 top right (Anna Clopet), 43 (Peter M. Fisher), 26 (Jim Mahoney/Dallas Morning News), 30 (Tom & Dee Ann McCarthy); Getty Images: 32 (Gary S. Chapman/Photographer's Choice), 40 left (Peter Dazeley/The Image Bank), 40 bottom right, 41 bottom (Nicholas Eveleigh/Iconica), 4, 5 (Patrick McDonogh), 10 (Thinkstock Images), 25 (Gavin R. Wilson/Photonica); Media Bakery: back cover background, cover main (Chad Baker), back cover foreground (Steve Weisbauer), 13, 20, 21; Photo Researchers, NY: 41 top left (BSIP), 40 center (David Hay Jones/SPL), 41 top center (Will & Deni McIntyre/SPL), 22 (Phillipe Psaila), 18, 24, 28 (Tek Image/SPL); ShutterStock, Inc.: 42 bottom (Blamb), 31 (BMCL), 14, 15 (corepics), cover inset, 44, 45 (John Schwegel), 42 top (sgame); The Innocence Project: 27 center left, 27 left; Virginia Department of Forensic Science/Jennifer Bertelsen: 38.

Library of Congress Cataloging-in-Publication Data
Prokos, Anna.
DNA doesn't lie : is the real criminal behind bars? / Anna Prokos.
p. cm.
Includes bibliographical references and index.
ISBN-13 978-0-545-32800-5
ISBN-10 0-545-32800-4
1. Cowans, Stephan—Trials, litigation, etc.
2. DNA fingerprinting—Law and legislation—United States.
3. Judicial error—United States. I. Title.
KF224.C686P76 2011
363.25'62—dc2   2011005977

Copyright © 2012, 2007 Scholastic Inc.

All Rights Reserved. Published by Scholastic Inc. Printed in the U.S.A.

SCHOLASTIC, XBOOKS, and associated logos are trademarks and/or registered trademarks of Scholastic Inc.

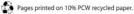 Pages printed on 10% PCW recycled paper.

6 7 8 9 10   40   21 20 19 18 17 16

DNA DOESN'T LIE

Is the Real Criminal Behind Bars?

ANNA PROKOS

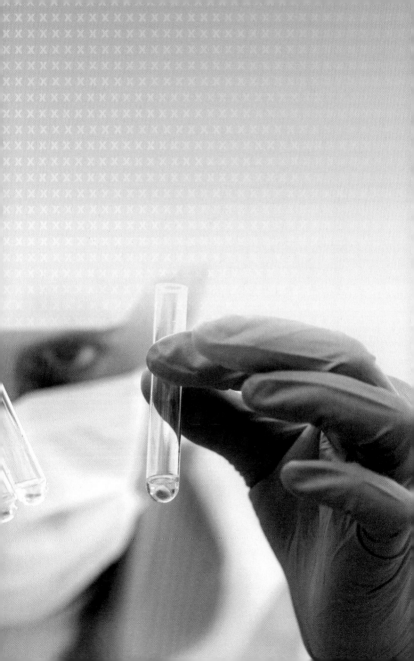

TABLE OF CONTENTS

1

Case Closed?

**A jury hands down its verdict.
Has the right man been convicted?**

On May 30, 1997, police sergeant Gregory Gallagher was on duty in Boston, Massachusetts. From inside his squad car, he spotted a man he thought looked suspicious. Gallagher got out of his car. As he did, the man ran. Gallagher pursued him.

In the backyard of a house, they wrestled, and the man grabbed Gallagher's gun. He shot Gallagher twice, once in the back and once in the thigh. He also shot at an eyewitness who was watching from a nearby window.

The shooter ran from the scene, leaving only a baseball cap behind. Then he broke into a nearby house and demanded a drink of water from the terrified residents. He took off his sweatshirt and put down the gun. After drinking his water, he put down the cup, left the house, and disappeared.

Solid Evidence?

Two weeks later, Gallagher identified 26-year-old Stephan Cowans from a set of photographs. The police arrested Cowans.

Prosecutors thought they had enough evidence to charge Cowans with attempted murder. The eyewitness from the window had picked him out of a lineup. And experts claimed that a fingerprint found on the cup the attacker had drunk from on the day of the shooting matched Cowans's left thumb.

On July 6, a jury found Cowans guilty of assault and battery of a police officer. He was sentenced to 30 to 45 years in jail. But Cowans insisted he was innocent. And he was determined to prove it.

Crime Scene Investigators

Here's a step-by-step guide to investigating a crime scene.

1. Do a walk-through. Take note of everything before you collect any evidence. Look for how the criminal may have gotten into and out of the area.

2. Protect the crime scene. Lots of people work at a crime scene: photographers, police, medical examiners, sketch artists, fire fighters, and reporters. Make sure they don't touch important evidence.

3. Pick a path. Choose one path into and out of a crime scene. Make sure everyone uses it. This helps protect any possible evidence.

4. Record it. Take pictures of the scene. Videotape it. Sketch it if you have to. And be sure to measure bloodstains.

5. Collect fragile materials first. Fingerprints, footprints, hairs, and fibers can get stepped on, blown away, or smudged. It's important to find them and collect them quickly.

6. Don't flush! Don't use the toilet or turn on faucets. You could be sending important evidence down the drain.

15

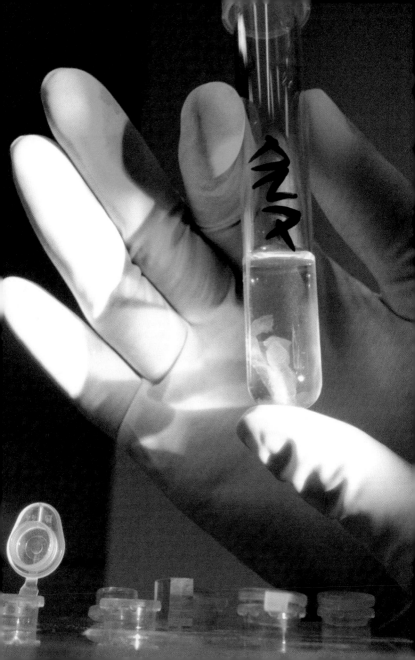

2

DNA on the Case

DNA evidence can lock up the guilty—and free the innocent.

From inside his jail cell, Stephan Cowans was determined to prove his innocence. He contacted an organization called the Innocence Project.

The Innocence Project was formed in 1992. Its goal is to use DNA evidence to free innocent prisoners.

What's DNA? DNA is a chain of molecules found in almost every cell of your body. (A molecule is a group of atoms. Atoms are the basic building blocks of all things.) Everyone has a unique set of DNA.

A FORENSIC INVESTIGATOR takes a blood sample at a crime scene. The blood will be analyzed for DNA, which can be compared to the DNA of a suspect of the crime.

18

DNA Evidence

In 1984, scientist Alec Jeffreys figured out how to identify a person's unique DNA profile. His discoveries were soon incorporated into police work. DNA evidence was used for the first time in a U.S. criminal court in 1987. The DNA from the suspect's bodily fluids proved that he had done the crime.

Since then, forensic detectives—specialists who use science to help solve crimes—have searched crime scenes and victims for DNA evidence. There's DNA in skin, hair, blood, saliva, and other body fluids. When a suspect's DNA is found at a crime scene or on a victim, it can prove the suspect's guilt.

The founders of the Innocence Project realized that DNA could also be used to prove someone's innocence. The group arranged for DNA tests on evidence from cases they suspected had been decided incorrectly. These tests have freed more than 250 innocent people from prison.

Could DNA evidence free Stephan Cowans?

The World's Smallest Instruction Manual

What makes you so special? The answer is in your DNA.

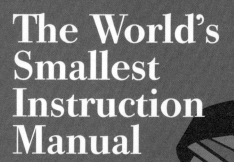

What is DNA?
It's a long chain of molecules that contains the instructions—called genes—that all living things need in order to function.

What does DNA stand for?
Deoxyribonucleic acid (see glossary for pronunciation).

What does it do?
DNA determines what you look like and how your body works. It controls everything from the color of your eyes to how tall you will be.

Where is my DNA?
There's a copy of your DNA in almost every cell in your body. That means that just about every cell has a complete set of instructions for making another you!

So my DNA is a lot different from everyone else's?
Sort of. If you compared two people's DNA, you'd see that they're 99.9% the same. Only 0.1% is different. That's the part that makes you *you*. And that's the part that scientists use to identify a person.

How long does DNA last?
It can break down in the hot sun, humidity, or rain. But under the right conditions, DNA can survive a long time. DNA has been found in ancient Egyptian mummies!

3

Questionable Evidence

The Innocence Project takes the case.

In 2000, Stephan Cowans finally caught a lucky break. His case landed on the desk of Robert N. Feldman of the New England Innocence Project. Just like the original Innocence Project, it uses DNA evidence to try to exonerate—prove the innocence of—people who were wrongly convicted.

Feldman's team of lawyers looked at Cowans's case. They found several holes in it.

Holes in the Case

First, not all the witnesses had identified Cowans as the attacker. The people in the house the attacker had broken into had gotten a good look at him. But they hadn't picked Cowans out of a lineup.

Second, several items that the attacker had touched were never tested for DNA. The attacker had left the gun and his baseball cap and sweatshirt when he fled. Some of those items could have sweat on them, which can contain DNA.

Third, the police had relied on two eyewitnesses,

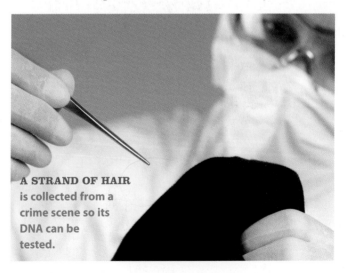

A STRAND OF HAIR is collected from a crime scene so its DNA can be tested.

DNA Dos and Don'ts

To crime scene investigators, DNA evidence is as precious as gold. The right evidence can help convict a criminal or clear an innocent person. Here are some dos and don'ts for handling DNA evidence.

- **Do** wear gloves and masks when handling DNA.

- **Don't** breathe, spit, or sneeze on the evidence. You don't want your own DNA to mix with the sample!

- **Do** document the crime scene. Make notes about where and when evidence was found. Take photographs of the scene. Then store the evidence in a safe place.

- **Don't** expose samples to humidity, direct sunlight, or rain. These conditions can break down the chemicals that hold DNA together.

- **Do** keep a chain-of-custody report. This shows who has handled the evidence. Everyone who touches the evidence must sign it. The chain-of-custody report can be used in court. It helps prove that no one has tampered with evidence.

Not Guilty!

DNA evidence can give innocent prisoners a second chance at life.

Sometimes people go to jail for crimes they didn't commit. That's why Barry Scheck and Peter Neufeld formed the Innocence Project in 1992.

In the past 20 years, DNA evidence has freed more than 250 people in the United States who served time for crimes they didn't commit. Here's a look at four of them.

FREED PRISONER
Larry Fuller (center) with attorneys Vanessa Potkin and Barry Scheck

Gallagher and the man in the window. Eyewitnesses often make mistakes. In fact, mistakes are common when eyewitnesses identify people who are racially different from themselves. Cowans was black. The eyewitnesses were white.

And fourth, the police had also based their case on the fingerprint found on the water cup. However, the print may have been unreliable, too. It was only part of a fingerprint—what experts call a partial.

name: Maurice Patterson
convicted: 2003
charge: murder
released: 2010

name: Miguel Roman
convicted: 1990
charge: murder
released: 2008

name: Frank Sterling
convicted: 1992
charge: murder
released: 2010

name: Antonio Beaver
convicted: 1997
charge: robbery
released: 2007

On the Case

Feldman and his staff decided to take the case.

The Innocence Project lawyers had two questions to answer. Did the attacker leave any DNA evidence at the scene? If so, did it match Cowans's DNA?

Feldman asked the court to have the evidence from Cowans's case released to a lab for DNA testing. Forensic scientists would find out whether Cowans's DNA profile matched any DNA on the evidence.

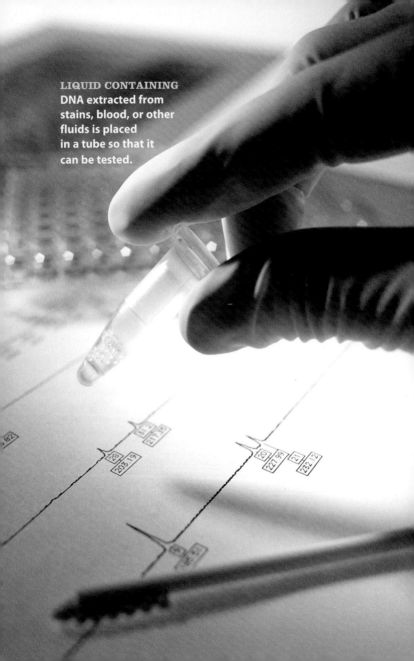

LIQUID CONTAINING DNA extracted from stains, blood, or other fluids is placed in a tube so that it can be tested.

4

Testing, Testing

Can Stephan Cowans prove his innocence?

In May 2003, the court agreed to provide the evidence that Robert Feldman requested. By then, Stephan Cowans had been in jail for nearly six years.

Fortunately, the DNA from the evidence in Cowans's case had not spoiled. Scientists at the crime lab found sweat on the brim of the baseball hat. They also collected traces of saliva from the cup. Both samples produced enough DNA to test.

A SCIENTIST ANALYZES a DNA profile. The pattern of bands in a DNA profile is unique for every person.

Scientists then created a DNA profile from each sample. They also processed a sample of saliva from Cowans.

DNA Saves the Day

Now it was time to compare the samples. Scientists lined up the DNA profiles. The DNA profiles from the baseball cap and the glass were the same. But they didn't match Cowans's DNA profile.

To make sure, the court had the sweatshirt tested. The DNA from the sweatshirt matched the DNA from the cap and cup exactly. But none of the samples matched Cowans's DNA profile.

Cowans's lawyers had proved what they had suspected all along. Their client Stephen Cowans had not attacked and shot Sergeant Gallagher.

Cowans was an innocent man.

THE ATTACKER had left his baseball cap in the backyard where he shot Sergeant Gallagher.

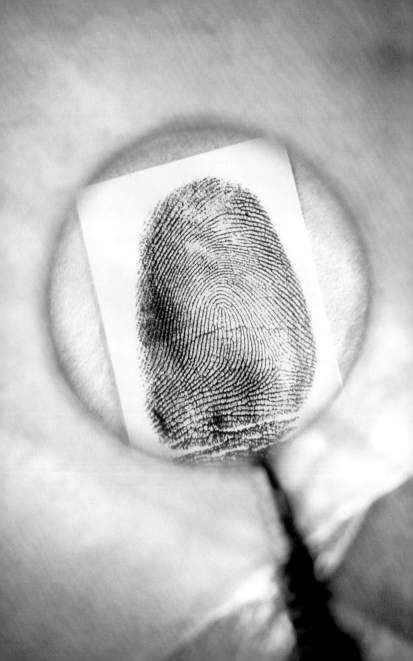

5

Justice–and an Apology

The police take another look at the fingerprint.

Stephan Cowans's lawyer presented the DNA evidence to a judge and asked for a new trial. David E. Meier was the county assistant district attorney. He represented the government in criminal trials. He did not argue with the request for a new trial. The judge scheduled it for January 21, 2004.

In the meantime, Meier got an expert to look again at the fingerprint that had been found on the cup that the attacker had drunk from. This time, the expert said the print on the cup did not match Cowans's thumbprint. Two days later, prosecutors admitted their mistake.

Free at Last

The judge decided there was no need for a new trial. He freed Cowans that day.

On January 23, Stephan Cowans walked out of prison to join his family. "I don't think there are any words in the dictionary to describe what that's like," he said.

The acting Boston police commissioner publicly apologized to Cowans. "Our error contributed to Mr. Cowans's conviction," he said. "For this we offer him and his family our sincere apology."

STEPHAN COWANS, shown here with his cousin, was released from prison after serving six years for a crime he didn't commit.

In August 2006, the City of Boston paid Cowans a reported $3.2 million to settle a civil lawsuit brought against the city.

Tragically, just over a year later, in October 2007, Cowans was shot dead in his home in Randolph, Massachusetts. He had been free for three years and was rebuilding his life.

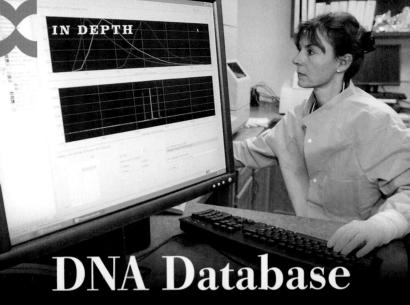

DNA Database

**Just like DNA, CODIS is packed
with information.**

Say you're a police investigator. You go to a crime scene
and find some evidence. You take it back to the lab. The DNA
experts say that you've got a great sample of the offender's
DNA. They just don't know *who* the offender is. You still have
to find a suspect.

Wouldn't it be great if there were an easier way?

There is. In 1998, the Federal Bureau of Investigation
created a DNA database. It's called CODIS. That stands for
Combined DNA Index System.

CODIS contains DNA samples from more than 6 million
people. Some states enter only the samples of convicted
criminals. Other states enter people's samples when they're
arrested.

These days, laws in all 50 states support CODIS. Anyone
convicted of a sex offense or murder must have his or her
DNA entered into the system.

X FILES

A Chain of Evidence

Forensic scientist Ann Pollard is an expert DNA profiler.

ANN POLLARD is a DNA scientist for the Virginia Department of Forensic Science.

What is your job?

POLLARD: I do DNA analysis on evidence in criminal cases. I also supervise a group of other scientists and lab assistants who do the same.

What kind of training did you have?

POLLARD: I have my bachelor of science degree in biology. I also have a master's degree in criminal justice, with a specialization in forensic science [the scientific study of the evidence of a crime]. I took a ten-month training program in forensic biology and DNA analysis.

What's a typical day like on the job?

POLLARD: I could be working on 15 to 20 cases at a time. I take one case at a time. I might spend two or three days sitting in the lab. I go through evidence, get samples ready, and stuff like that. Then, I'll spend another week doing actual DNA analysis. Next, I'll write up all the reports and paperwork.

What's the hardest thing for you?

POLLARD: I'd have to say interpreting DNA profiles. We have all these mixtures of samples. And we have to figure out whose DNA it is. People's lives depend on it.

What's the coolest part about your job?

POLLARD: I get to work on something different all the time. Sometimes, I get basic cases, like finding DNA from a bloodstain or cigarette butt. But every once in a while I get to work on cool stuff, like finding DNA from cans or bottles, guns, hats, clothing, steering wheels— you name it.

What can middle school and high school kids do to get started in the field?

POLLARD: Look for colleges that offer good forensic science programs. It's also important for the school to offer in-depth lab work in the field you want to work in. That way you can get hands-on experience.

DNA Detectives

Check out DNA specialists' tools of the trade.

AT THE CRIME SCENE:

1 Swab kit: Police use a swab to collect cells from the inside of a person's cheek. Then they seal the swab in an envelope.

2 Tyvek suit: Tyvek is a strong, waterproof material. Investigators wear Tyvek suits when they need protection from dangerous substances.

IN THE LAB:

3 FMBIO: This scanning machine uses a laser to cause the DNA to give off light. The light is then turned into an image in bar code form.

4 Electrophoresis system: This machine separates long strands of DNA from short strands. This helps scientists find the part of the DNA they need to examine.

5 Thermal cycler:
This machine allows scientists to duplicate small samples of DNA through a process called polymerase chain reaction (PCR). It is one of the most important developments in forensic science since the discovery of DNA.

AT THE SCENE AND IN THE LAB:

6 Latex gloves: These protect investigator's hands from exposure to blood and other samples. They keep the investigator from contaminating the evidence.

7 Scalpel: A sharp knife that's used to scrape up dried fluids for testing.

In Your Genes

DNA determines what *you* look like. But what does *DNA* look like?

When scientists do DNA profiling, they work with materials that are far too small to see with the naked eye. But if you *could* see them, here's what they would look like.

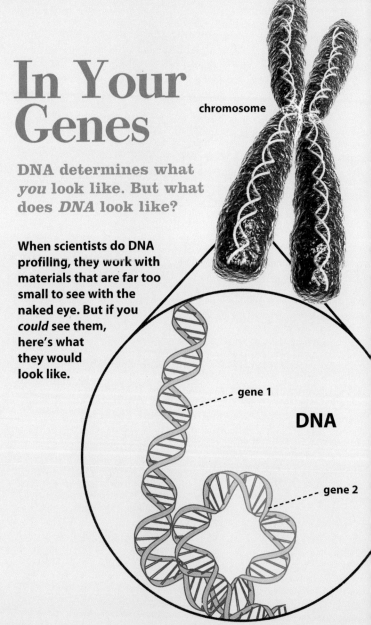

chromosome

gene 1

DNA

gene 2

Genes

Your body is made up of trillions of cells. Inside almost every cell are "sets of instructions" called genes. Genes determine a person's traits—how each person looks and functions. Humans have about 30,000 genes.

DNA

Genes are strung together in long strands of material called DNA. A strand of DNA is shaped like a twisted ladder, or helix.

Chromosomes

A chromosome is made up of a very long, coiled-up strand of DNA. In humans, there are 23 pairs of chromosomes in almost every cell in the body. You get half your chromosomes from your mother and half from your father. So you get some of your traits from each parent. For example, you might have your father's black hair and your mother's blue eyes.

Seeing Double

Do twins have the same DNA?

Identical twins look almost exactly the same. And their DNA is exactly the same, too. So what happens if a twin commits a crime? DNA can't be used to determine which twin is innocent and which twin is guilty.

Luckily for investigators, identical twins don't share the same fingerprints. So prints left at the crime scene can determine which twin did the crime.

RESOURCES

Here's a selection of books and websites for more information about DNA analysis and forensic science.

What to Read Next

NONFICTION

Ballard, Carol. *At the Crime Scene! Collecting Clues and Evidence*. Berkeley Heights, NJ: Enslow Publishers, 2009.

Beres, D. B., and Anna Prokos. *Dusting and DNA*. New York: Scholastic, 2008.

Cooper, Christopher. *Forensic Science* (DK Eyewitness Books). New York: DK Publishing, 2008.

Fridell, Ron. *DNA Fingerprinting: The Ultimate Identity*. New York: Franklin Watts, 2001.

Nardo, Don. *DNA Evidence*. Detroit: Lucent Books, 2008.

Platt, Richard. *Crime Scene: The Ultimate Guide to Forensic Science*. New York: DK Publishing, 2003.

Prokos, Anna. *Guilty by a Hair! Real-Life DNA Matches!* New York: Scholastic, 2007.

Rainis, Kenneth G. *Blood and DNA Evidence: Crime-Solving Science Experiments*. Berkeley Heights, NJ: Enslow Publishers, 2006.

Shulz, Karen K. *CSI Expert! Forensic Science for Kids*. Waco, TX: Prufrock Press Inc., 2008.

FICTION

Ferguson, Alane. *The Angel of Death: A Forensic Mystery*. New York: Sleuth/Viking, 2006.

Hein, E.K. *The Forensic Mission: Investigate Forensic Science Through a Killer Mystery!* Hoboken, NJ: Wiley Publishing Inc., 2007.

Reichs, Kathy. *Virals*. New York: Razorbill, 2011.

Websites

CSI: The Experience:
Web Adventures
http://forensics.rice.edu
This site, part of an educational
exhibit that has traveled to science
museums around the country,
immerses you in hands-on science
while leading you through the
challenge of solving a crime
mystery.

FBI Kids' Page
**http://www.fbi.gov/
fun-games/kids/kids**
The FBI's website for kids tells how
the FBI conducts investigations.

Forensic Files
http://www.forensicfiles.com
Learn about real cases featured on
the truTV show and go behind the
scenes.

Forensic Science
**http://library.thinkquest.
org/04oct/00206/**
This site provides an in-depth look
at what happens at a crime scene
and how an investigation works.

The Innocence Project
www.innocenceproject.org
The official site of the Innocence
Project provides information on
specific cases in which DNA
evidence has proved a convict's
innocence. The site also discusses
the causes of incorrect rulings and
ways to fix them.

Young Forensic
Scientists Forum
http://www2.aafs.org/yfsf
This is the site for the Young
Forensic Scientists Forum, part
of the American Academy of
Forensic Sciences. It has all kinds
of information about the field of
forensics and ways to get involved.

GLOSSARY

assault (uh-SAWLT) *noun*
a threat or attempt to strike another, whether successful or not

battery (BAT-uh-ree) *noun* the actual intentional striking of someone, even if the injury is slight

biology (bye-OL-uh-jee) *noun* the scientific study of living things

cell (SEL) *noun* the basic structural unit of all living things

chromosomes (KROH-muh-sohmz) *noun* threadlike structures in the center of a cell; they are made of DNA and contain all your genetic information

civil lawsuit (SIV-il LAW-soot) *noun* a legal action brought by one party against another with the goal of winning damages (usually a sum of money) for injury or wrongdoing

convicted (kuhn-VIK-tid) *adjective* found guilty of a crime

database (DAY-tuh-bayss) *noun* information that is organized and stored in a computer

defendant (di-FEN-duhnt) *noun* the person in a court case who has been accused of a crime

district attorney (DISS-trikt uh-TUR-nee) *noun* a lawyer who represents a city or town in criminal trials

DNA (DEE-en-ay) *noun* the genetic material contained in cells; it's the set of instructions for your body. *DNA* is the abbreviation for *deoxyribonucleic acid* (dye-OK-si-rye-bow-nu-KLAY-ik ASS-id)

DNA profiling (DEE-en-ay PROH-fyl-ing) *noun* a process by which DNA is extracted from a sample of blood, saliva, or other fluid or tissue so that it can be compared with other DNA samples; also called DNA testing or genetic fingerprinting

evidence (EHV-uh-denss) *noun* materials gathered in an investigation to help prove someone's guilt or innocence

expert (EX-purt) *noun* someone who knows a lot about a particular subject

extract (ek-STRAKT) *verb* to take or pull something out

eyewitness (eye-WIT-ness) *noun* a person who saw a crime being committed

forensic (fuh-REN-zik) *adjective* describing the science used to investigate and solve crimes

gene (jeen) *noun* a single part within a DNA chain that contains one unit of information

identical twins (eye-DEN-tih-kuhl TWINZ) *noun* twins who developed from the splitting of a single fertilized egg; identical twins are born with the same DNA

jury (JU-ree) *noun* a group of people at a trial who listen to a court case and decide whether a person is guilty or innocent

lineup (LYNE-uhp) *noun* a line of people shown to the eyewitness of a crime. If the witness can pick the suspect out of the lineup, the witness's evidence will count as evidence at the trial

molecule (MOL-uh-kyool) *noun* the smallest part of a substance that displays all the chemical properties of that substance

polymerase chain reaction (puh-LIM-uh-rase chayn ree-AK-shun) *noun* a process that allows scientists to duplicate small amounts of DNA

prosecutor (PROSS-uh-kyoo-tur) *noun* a lawyer who represents the government in criminal trials

pursue (pur-SOO) *verb* to follow or chase someone

suspect (SUS-pekt) *noun* a person who law enforcement officials think might be guilty of a crime

testify (TESS-tuh-fye) *verb* to state the truth or give evidence in court

verdict (VUR-dikt) *noun* a decision from a jury about someone's guilt or innocence